Breaths We Called Words

Aurora Jewkes

BookLeaf Publishing

India | USA | UK

Presentation by *BookLeaf Publishing*

Web: www.bookleafpub.com

E-mail: info@bookleafpub.com

ISBN: 9789357215718

First edition 2022

PREFACE

I wrote this, hoping one day you'd read it and understand.

Ion

We stand between the atoms and the stars.
The molecules that run through me once ran
through you.
It can be said we are breathing each other,
You and I.

Our atoms are immortal.
Once I depart from this life, they will move into
something new.
Maybe this ensuing person will love your
ensuing soul.
Maybe our atoms then could become molecules.

It turns out, we were just mixtures.
We combined without ever chemically bonding.
To be separated once again into our original
components.
Never meant to connect.

I was certain we were an atom.
"undivided"
Yet, we split in two.
Now there's only me; only you.

I feel

That hurt my feelings,
but in every brilliant way.

It hurt in the sense
as every meaningful thing should.

It has weight
As gravity pulls on every human experience.

Systems Reject Radical Change

The broken love the broken
Perfect the perfect
The abused love the abuse

The honest love the honest
Damaged the damage
You're not a One I can choose

I put a hand to my chest and
hope for the best
that I can feel it beating

No matter how I press there's no
touching the mess
This blood-red box is missing

Our Era

To be rich and guilty
To be poor and innocent.
To be judged by folly
To increase incarceration.

Where the young boy was born
wearing the wrong shade,
To be tried as an adult
Barely surpassing seventh grade.

It isn't whether they
Deserve to die.
That's not in our will.
But it is rather if we
Contain the right -
Deserve to kill.

Are we more than the worst
We have done?
After time and remorse
Only goodbyes to their sons.

Well after the gavel
Their trial remains.
But these problems cease to be mine
When I look away.

Our survival is rooted
In the survival of each one.
Not leaving out the poor
To a systematic corporation.

It is necessary to be brave.
To be aware, to embrace
All of the suffering,
And become enraged.

When we stand for humanity,
When the injustices wash away,
When I can see no inequalities
To which I'll forever pray.

To the poor sentenced guilty.
And the rich deemed innocent
Judged by our follies
Conformed by incarceration.

And thus continues
The era of our terrorism.

Mistakes Were Made

My first mistake was falling for someone who was right-handed.

Carthartic

A splash entangled in a water web of emotion
Plasters the cheeks of a distressed soul.
Where is the grief, where is the pain?
Hidden behind her faltering smile?

Plasters the cheeks of a distressed soul.
it drips into the corners of her mouth
Hidden behind her faltering smile
She swims in the puddles around her.

It drips into the corners of her mouth
Streaks paint her breaking face
She swims in the puddles around her
Feeling her eyes will forever be stained.

Streaks paint her breaking face
Breathing isn't an option
Feeling her eyes will forever be stained.
They glisten, begging to be set free.

Breathing isn't an option.
Neither sense is allowed to exist.
They glisten, begging to be set free.
Her eyes melt in a sea of damage.

Neither sense is allowed to exist.
Her voice will have no sound.
Her eyes melt in a sea of damage.
Those tears remain.

Her voice will have no sound.
A splash entangled in a water web of emotion.
Those tears remain.
Where is the grief? Where is the pain?

Promise of a Rainbow

Clouds form in place;
droplets suffocating in sorrow;
thunder from past mistakes;
puddles of death and shame;
tormented tears fogged in shadow;
yet there's always,
the promise of a rainbow

Lover's Ledge

There is this ledge.
Where the brave go,
Where the young leap,
Where the desperate fall.

There is this cliff.
Hoping at the bottom,
A suitor awaits.
Hoping by the end,
A miracle, you'll be saved.

There are some
Who dangle their feet,
Who's eyes linger in the abyss,
Those who cling by their fingers.
And others who sit at a distance.

And then there are they
Who run.
They don't hesitate.
They don't fear.
And lover's leap takes.

But it can hurt to fall.
At times they can promise,
"Don't worry, I'll catch."
And sidestep before
You land.

And all that's left are
Shattered pieces at
The foundation of this ridge.
And somehow, in some way
You have to put yourself
Back together
Before you can fall again.

But why fall for someone
who isn't going to be there
to catch you?
You pray for that One.

Sometimes we have to
run and jump
and suffer the consequences.

All before this ledge.

4am

Late again.
But you say it's okay.
You say it's alright because it was your decision
to stay.
You always chose to remain.
Until that one time, you didn't.

The Wonderful

I notice the acts of tenderness you give.

The elderly woman you assist
The compliment you gave to that outcasted
stranger
The prayers you spoke for your hurting
neighbors

I notice.

I admire the resilience you encompass.

Forgiving once again
Putting on that fighting grin
Brawling those battles within
Even when there is every right not to.

I see you.

It's easy to forget
The wonderful you are.

DNA

In my genetic strands
Lie the cursed parts of me
That will not ever atone

My destiny to become my parents.
To be silenced
To be lifeless
To never be loved.

My prospect to become my aunts.
To be abused
To be used
To never be enough.

My future to become my grandmother.
To be deserted
To be discarded
To not be cared of

My inevitability to become me
To be forgotten
To be heartbroken
To never measure up

In my genetic strands
Lie the cursed parts of me
That will not ever atone

In my genetic strands
Lie my undeniable belief
That I'm meant to be alone

Mesolimbic System

You are what converted me
Hijack mind with dopamine

Needle
Swallow
Shot

Overcome the habitual maim
Bruise the mark of gain

Numbness
Blackness
Lost

I waged to quit temptation
But fell to your enslavement

Labels
Stigma
Fraud

Cravings for the disease
Can't save me from me

Attempt
Relapse
God

I long for human connection
But succumb to addiction

Words

Words.
They don't belong to you once you've said them
They become captives to the ears that heard
them
Until we're all beggars.

Words.
Powerful design.
That's how the world was manufactured.
Yet you used them to disfigure mine.
Desolate in the fires.

Words.
Fragmented sounds placed to assemble meaning
from nothing
To construct me into something
But I was only broken letters.

Words.
How you knew not of their weight,
Misunderstood your sincerity bait
An unforseen enfetter.

Words.
I can't count the syllables,
Can't number the synonyms
In which you played the victim
Some things don't get better.

My words, yours.
Although you may forget
I will only remember
The words.

Body

Wrap in cellophane
Drown in iron and weight
To eliminate
The self-hate, tissue scars,
And imposed pain

Measure in caution tape
Nausea echos and it takes
As I pray
The man-made, warrior marks
To love those parts away

Truce of 1914

Fragments of cartilage,
Torn uniforms
Wisps of crimson bandages.

Enclosed by the wire,
Shrapnel mud
Collapsed sands of damages.

Only hope of leave
Ends with lead in its bloodstream
Only limbs of keep
Lie in its deceasing feet

Amidst a shadowed trough
Can darkness spare a day?
As enemies' carols ring
They'll walk to meet halfway

With each foot forward
They step onto No Man's Land
Holding the artillery fire
To shake the combatant's hand

Laughing with those who
Flamed their weakest brother
Yet remembering too,
How mercy shall be their finisher

For one day ceased the machines
A forgiving spirit ensued
In the War to end all Wars,
The Christmas Truce

What Makes Me Laugh

I laugh at the way I trip over nothing
How to fall on the stairs is up
That kiss we shared was Netwon's law
Leaving bruising on the lip

I laugh at the notes that you sing
How the waves move in a VHS
That scratch noise on my vinyl
Leaving fingerprints on broken disks

I laugh at the spilled milk in the morning
How time travels without my consent
That top hat latched in the cobblestone
Leaving everyone else to forget

I laugh at the burden I'm bearing
How chocolate heals most of it
That mathematical equation of life
Leaving out how much it meant

Red Light Green Light

Driving in overcast of the past
The streetlights come into view.

Yellow.
I slow, slow myself out of denial.
I fell for you
as gravity had me land on the brake pedal.

Emotional flicker
Moments away until
Strangers

Red.
Haunted at the shaking beam.
I simply grieve
Tormented by your leave, break to scream.

Enduring Character
Hope removed my
Barriers

Green.
I don't know how to let go.
I only know how to carry on
Pretending my foot isn't still on the brake.

At this intersection,
I played the game.

And I Accelerate.

Eviction

Wooden creek
Dust tangles in blackness
The shades are drawn

Silver cheek
Matter dangles in desolation
Strand of light gone

Epithet

Known as the creature in the home
The hauntings begin.
Sang silent, and silence bled.

The Terrible,
The Great.
For name's sake
Slaughtered his Son.
My Savior,
My Christ.
For sins did Forsake
Slaughter was the Son

Thereby named the poltergeist in our place
Whisperers and soothsayers
Yelled anger, and anger fled.

Of Almost

A fragment scarce
Of forever
Belt loops erased distance
One who checked
My made-up boxes,
Gone from my
Existence.
It aches more than
A lover of longer
The promises
Of phantom Ghost
Two wanderers
Of Almost.

Pardon

Perhaps the reason I can't write this
I don't want to change
And accept letting go,
I'd rather someone to blame

But God Forgives.
It's what the scriptures spake
To alllow Seventy Times Seven
Was His price to pay

My valves can't compensate
Where is my Balm?
This forgotten spirit
Engraved in His palms.

Anger unrestrained
Stubborn legality motions
Red and Blue lights
Is this something I can pardon?

This myriad hamartia
Calloused bloody chance
Battered black bruises
Am I to hold out the Olive Branch?

By His unfaltering grace
With my hammer and glue
I'll learn to repaint
Hope for walls to say,

I forgive you.